MUR THE STUDIO

by Agatha Christie

SAMUEL FRENCH

Copyright © 1937, 1948, 1954 Agatha Christie Limited. All Rights Reserved. 'AGATHA CHRISTIE', 'POIROT', the Agatha Christie Signature and the AC Monogram logo are registered trademarks of Agatha Christie Limited in the UK and elsewhere. All Rights Reserved..

MURDER IN THE STUDIO is fully protected under the copyright laws of the British Commonwealth, including Canada, the United States of America, and all other countries of the Copyright Union. All rights, including professional and amateur stage productions, recitation, lecturing, public reading, motion picture, radio broadcasting, television, online/digital production, and the rights of translation into foreign languages are strictly reserved.

ISBN 978-0-573-13016-8

www.concordtheatricals.co.uk
www.concordtheatricals.com
www.agathachristielimited.com

FOR PRODUCTION ENQUIRIES
UNITED KINGDOM AND WORLD
EXCLUDING NORTH AMERICA
licensing@concordtheatricals.co.uk
020-7054-7200
NORTH AMERICA
info@concordtheatricals.com
1-866-979-0447

Each title is subject to availability from Concord Theatricals, depending upon country of performance.

CAUTION: Professional and amateur producers are hereby warned that *MURDER IN THE STUDIO* is subject to a licensing fee. The purchase, renting, lending or use of this book does not constitute a licence to perform this title(s), which licence must be obtained from the appropriate agent prior to any performance. Performance of this title(s) without a licence is a violation of copyright law and may subject the producer and/or presenter of such performances to penalties. Both amateurs and professionals considering a production are strongly advised to apply to the appropriate agent before starting rehearsals, advertising, or booking a theatre. A licensing fee must be paid whether the title is presented for charity or gain and whether or not admission is charged.

This work is published by Samuel French, an imprint of Concord Theatricals. Ltd

For all enquiries regarding motion picture, television, and other media rights, please contact Concord Theatricals.

No one shall make any changes in this title for the purpose of production. No part of this book may be reproduced, stored in a retrieval system, scanned, uploaded, or transmitted in any form, by any means, now known or yet to be invented, including mechanical, electronic, digital, photocopying, recording, videotaping, or otherwise, without the prior written permission of the publisher. No one shall share this title, or part of this title, to any social media or file hosting websites.

The moral right of Agatha Christie to be identified as author of this work has been asserted in accordance with Section 77 of the Copyright, Designs and Patents Act 1988.

USE OF COPYRIGHTED MUSIC

A licence issued by Concord Theatricals to perform this play does not include permission to use the incidental music specified in this publication. In the United Kingdom: Where the place of performance is already licensed by the PERFORMING RIGHT SOCIETY (PRS) a return of the music used must be made to them. If the place of performance is not so licensed then application should be made to PRS for Music (www.prsformusic.com). A separate and additional licence from PHONOGRAPHIC PERFORMANCE LTD (www. ppluk.com) may be needed whenever commercial recordings are used. Outside the United Kingdom: Please contact the appropriate music licensing authority in your territory for the rights to any incidental music.

USE OF COPYRIGHTED THIRD-PARTY MATERIALS

Licensees are solely responsible for obtaining formal written permission from copyright owners to use copyrighted third-party materials (e.g., artworks, logos) in the performance of this play and are strongly cautioned to do so. If no such permission is obtained by the licensee, then the licensee must use only original materials that the licensee owns and controls. Licensees are solely responsible and liable for clearances of all third-party copyrighted materials, and shall indemnify the copyright owners of the play(s) and their licensing agent, Concord Theatricals Ltd., against any costs, expenses, losses and liabilities arising from the use of such copyrighted third-party materials by licensees.

IMPORTANT BILLING AND CREDIT REQUIREMENTS

If you have obtained performance rights to this title, please refer to your licensing agreement for important billing and credit requirements.

The three plays making up *MURDER IN THE STUDIO* were first written as plays for radio and performed on the BBC. They may be presented together in any order and either in "live radio" format or in a traditional stage presentation set in the locations of the scripts.

TABLE OF CONTENTS

Personal Call 7
Yellow Iris 39
Butter in a Lordly Dish 65

Personal Call

CHARACTERS

FAY
JAMES BRENT
PAM BRENT
MRS. LAMB
EVAN CURTIS
MARY CURTIS
MR. ENDERBY
INSPECTOR NARRACOTT
OPERATOR
STATION ANNOUNCER
FIRST PORTER
SECOND PORTER
WOMAN
MAN

PERSONAL CALL was first performed on the BBC Radio Light Programme on Monday, 31 May 1954 and produced by Ayton Whitaker. The cast was as follows:

FAY	Jessie Evans
JAMES BRENT	James McKechnie
PAM BRENT	Mary Wimbush
MRS. LAMB	Joan Sanderson
EVAN CURTIS	Hamilton Dyce
MARY CURTIS	Janet Burnell
MR. ENDERBY	Norman Chidgey
INSPECTOR NARRACOTT	Edgar Norfolk
WITH	Sulwen Morgan, Cyril Shaps, Peter Claughton, Dorothy Clement, Alan Reid, Hugh David, and Ruth Cracknell

Scene One

(The confused noises of a cocktail party are heard. For further dialogue see Appendix Chatter Band A.)

VOICES. *(Jumbled.)* "Hullo Pam, you're looking wonderful. Marriage seems to agree with you."

"Come on in, old man. So glad you could make it."

"Pam's about somewhere."

"Darling, have you heard about Mona?"

(A telephone rings. It is unheeded for a moment or two then MRS. LAMB, a housemaid, answers it.)

MRS. LAMB. 'Ullo, 'ullo... Yes, Kensington 34598... Wot? ... Just a moment, please. I can't 'ear you.

(A door shuts and the cocktail party fades into the background.)

'Ullo, yes?

OPERATOR. Can Mr. James Brent take a personal call, please, from Newton Abbot?

MRS. LAMB. I'll try and get 'old of 'im but there's a party going on.

(The door opens. A surge of noise. Scraps of conversation are heard. For further dialogue see Appendix Chatter Band B.)

VOICES. "Mary, it's lovely to see you. It's been simply ages."

"Hullo, Johnnie, you must meet my wife. She's somewhere about."

"Cocktail, or would you rather have sherry?"

MRS. LAMB. Please, sir – please –

JAMES. We certainly are, but how we're ever going to manage on this travelling allowance I don't – eh, what?

MRS. LAMB. You're wanted on the phone, sir.

JAMES. What now? Who is it?

MRS. LAMB. It's a personal call, sir, from something Abbot.

JAMES. People will ring up at the most inconvenient moments. John, get Mona another drink. Hullo, Lois, lovely to see you. Pam's about somewhere –

(The party noises fade as the door shuts.)

Hullo?

OPERATOR. Is that Mr. James Brent speaking personally?

JAMES. James Brent speaking.

OPERATOR. Just a moment, please.

*(The **OPERATOR** connects the call.)*

Go ahead please. Mr. Brent is waiting.

*(**FAY** is put through. Her voice sounds remote and rather unearthly.)*

FAY. Hullo James?

JAMES. Who's speaking?

FAY. Don't you know?

(She laughs, mockingly.)

It's Fay...

JAMES. Who did you say? Sorry, the line's bad and there's a lot of noise going on here.

*(**FAY** speaks again, sounding nearer.)*

FAY. It's Fay...

JAMES. *(Startled.)* What did you say?

FAY. It's Fay, James? Don't you remember?

(There is a pause.)

JAMES. *(Upset.)* Who are you? Where are you speaking from?

FAY. I'm at Newton Abbot station. Where you left me.

JAMES. What's that? *(Angrily.)* Who is this?

FAY. I told you. I'm Fay... You remember – Fay? I'm waiting for you to come and meet me.

JAMES. Meet you? What do you mean?

FAY. I'm waiting at the station. At Newton Abbot.

JAMES. Look here, one of us is mad. What are you talking about? And who are you?

FAY. How often have I got to tell you that I'm Fay!

JAMES. If this is a practical joke, let me tell you that it's a very heartless and silly one.

FAY. It isn't a joke, James. I'm here – waiting. You'll have to come.

JAMES. Look, this is absurd. How dare you pretend –

(The door opens. A surge of party noise. For dialogue see Appendix Chatter Band C.)

PAM. So that's where you are, darling. Telephoning! For goodness' sake come back, people are pouring in. We want some more cocktails mixed.

(Her voice becomes concerned.)

Why – darling. What is it?

(The telephone receiver is slammed down.)

JAMES. *(Furiously.)* A cruel, silly, practical joke! You'd think people had something better to do.

(The door is shut. The party noise fades.)

PAM. Darling, what is it? Who was it ringing up?

JAMES. *(Irritably.)* How should I know? But I'm going to try and find out.

(He picks up the telephone receiver and dials.)

Can you possibly carry on for a few minutes without me, Pam? I'll be along as soon as I can, my sweet.

PAM. Yes, of course.

(There is a pause.)

PAM. You're really upset, aren't you, darling? What did whoever it was say?

OPERATOR. Operator. Can I help you?

JAMES. Oh, operator, yes. My name's Brent. Kensington 34598. You put through a personal call to me just now. Can you tell me where it came from?... Yes... Yes... You'll ring me back?... As soon as you can...

> *(He replaces the telephone receiver.)*

Sorry Pam, but it really made me see red.

PAM. But who was it?

JAMES. I'll tell you all about it later. Do go now, darling. The party will be getting out of hand.

PAM. It's being a great success – that's really the trouble. All right, darling, I'll cope. But do come soon.

JAMES. Yes, I will.

> *(The door opens. Party noise is heard briefly before the door shuts and it fades. For dialogue see Appendix Chatter Band D.)*

(Softly.) Fay... I wasn't dreaming it, she said Fay. And it was her voice too... Who the devil can have been playing a trick on me?

> *(The telephone rings.* **JAMES** *answers it.)*

OPERATOR. Mr. James Brent?

JAMES. Yes.

OPERATOR. I have made enquiries. No personal call has been put through to you today.

JAMES. What? But I can assure you –

OPERATOR. No personal call has been put through to you.

> *(**JAMES** hangs up the telephone.)*

JAMES. *(Shaken.)* But I don't understand. I don't understand... I heard her...

> *(The door opens. Party noise is heard briefly before it closes.)*

PAM. *(Crossly.)* Really James, if you've finished telephoning you might come along. You just stand there looking as though someone had socked you on the head!

JAMES. I really am sorry, Pam. I'm with you.

PAM. Who was it who rang you up?

JAMES. Oh – just somebody trying to be funny.

PAM. What did he say?

(She has a slight change of tone.)

Or was it a she?

JAMES. I don't know... I mean, it was a she... It was nothing particular.

PAM. *(Uneasily.)* Darling, you're not leading a double life, I hope? I shouldn't like that at all.

*(**JAMES**' tone is a little forced.)*

JAMES. You're the only woman in my life, Pam. I can assure you of that.

PAM. You'd have to say so anyway! But something seems to have shattered your morale.

JAMES. *(Bitterly.)* I just don't like silly jokes.

PAM. Well come on, back to the scrimmage. By the way, I asked Evan and Mary in for bridge tomorrow. I haven't seen Mary for ages and one can't talk at a show like this. Is that all right?

JAMES. Yes dear, quite all right.

*(A swell of noise as **JAMES** and **PAM** rejoin the party. For further dialogue see Appendix Chatter Band E.)*

Hullo Evan, not seen you for ages. I hear you're coming in to bridge tomorrow? Good show...

(The party fades.)

Scene Two

(The sounds of a railway station. The scream of an express engine is heard rushing through the station.)

FIRST PORTER. Mind them cases, Joe.

FAY. Porter!

FIRST PORTER. Yes ma'am, what is it?

FAY. Please can you tell me where I can find –

> *(The sound of shunting trains briefly drowns out her voice.)*

FIRST PORTER. Sorry ma'am, couldn't hear you. What did you say?

FAY. The telephones?

FIRST PORTER. Out by the booking office. Over the bridge.

FAY. It's a trunk call I want.

FIRST PORTER. The first box.

FAY. Thank you.

SECOND PORTER. Hullo Bert? Seen a ghost?

FIRST PORTER. 'Tis funny, you saying that. That woman was asking me the way to the telephone boxes – reckon as I've seen her before somewhere. And seems to me as when I saw her, 'twas something to do with a death. I can't just call to mind –

> *(A train is heard coming into the station. The* **STATION ANNOUNCER** *calls.)*

ANNOUNCER. All stations to Plymouth stopping. Newton Abbot. Newton Abbot. From Plymouth. Stopping train to Plymouth.

> *(The station noises fade.)*

Scene Three

(JAMES, PAM, EVAN, and MARY are heard playing bridge.)

EVAN. And I've got the best heart and a trump.

PAM. That makes us two down. Sorry, James. Your deal, Mary.

MARY. Cut, please.

JAMES. Jumping to four spades was a bit rash, Pam.

PAM. I've had an awful head today. After the party yesterday, I suppose.

EVAN. Jolly good party, Pam.

MARY. Yes indeed. Evan and I drank far too much.

PAM. Oh, one must do something to cheer oneself up nowadays.

MARY. One heart.

JAMES. Three diamonds.

EVAN. No bid.

PAM. Four clubs.

(The telephone rings.)

Oh bother!

JAMES. Mrs. Lamb will answer it. What did you say, four clubs?

MARY. Double, four clubs.

JAMES. Four diamonds.

EVAN. Double, four diamonds.

PAM. No bid.

MARY. No bid.

(The door opens.)

PAM. Yes Mrs. Lamb. What is it?

MRS. LAMB. It's a personal call, sir, for you.

JAMES. *(Shaken.)* For me? *(Slowly.)* All right – I'll come.

PAM. Darling – you don't think –

JAMES. It's quite all right. Probably Smith, about that transfer.

> *(The door closes.)*

EVAN. Wonder whether it's still raining?

> *(He is heard pulling the curtains open.* **PAM** *and* **MARY** *speak confidentially.)*

PAM. You know, Mary, he got a personal call yesterday from somewhere or other, and it upset him dreadfully. He told me it was someone playing a silly joke on him, but wouldn't tell me what the joke was. You know, Mary, it really quite worried me.

MARY. Have you got an extension?

PAM. Yes, in my bedroom. Do you think –

MARY. *(Urgently.)* I would…

> *(***PAM*** speaks somewhat artificially to* **EVAN**.*)*

PAM. I must just run upstairs and powder my nose.

EVAN. You women…

> *(Fade.)*

Scene Four

(**JAMES** *is heard on the telephone.*)

JAMES. Hullo – yes?

OPERATOR. Just a moment, please.

> (*A click is heard as the calls are connected.*)

Go ahead – you're through.

FAY. James? It's me again.

JAMES. Fay!

FAY. Yes, Fay…

JAMES. Now look here, what's the meaning of all this! What kind of a game is it?

FAY. It's not a game, James.

JAMES. If you think you're going to get me rattled, you're not.

FAY. You needn't be so upset. I just want you to come and meet me.

JAMES. Meet you? Where?

FAY. At Newton Abbot, of course. That's where I am now.

JAMES. A likely story! I checked up last night, it may interest you to know that no call from Newton Abbot had ever been put through.

FAY. But I am at Newton Abbot. Wait, I'll push the door a little bit open. Then you can hear –

> (*The faint sounds of trains and station noises are heard.*)

FIRST PORTER. (*Distant.*) Newton Abbot. Newton Abbot. Exeter and Paddington only, this train for Exeter and Paddington only.

FAY. You hear?

JAMES. (*Shaken.*) I – I don't believe it.

FAY. Haven't you even noticed what time it is?

JAMES. What do you mean?

FAY. The time. It's a quarter past seven. Don't you remember?

JAMES. *(Hoarsely.)* Shut up.

FAY. How rough you are, James darling. But you do see what I mean, don't you?

> *(**JAMES**' voice breaks with emotion.)*

JAMES. I don't know what you're talking about. What the hell do you want anyway?

FAY. I want you to come and meet me here.

JAMES. Where?

FAY. Oh dear, have I got to open that door again? I told you before. I'm where you left me. And I can't leave there until you come.

JAMES. This has got to stop, I tell you! It's got to stop.

> *(The call clicks.)*

Hullo – hullo – hullo! Are you there?

> *(The receiver is slammed down.)*

Damn!

> *(Fade.)*

Scene Five

(**EVAN** *and* **MARY** *are heard talking.*)

EVAN. And I still feel, Mary, that kids don't really appreciate –

(*The door opens.*)

Hullo James, put through a successful deal?

JAMES. What deal?

EVAN. (*Facetiously.*) Or was it a bit more personal than that, old man?

JAMES. (*Shortly.*) Nothing important. Where's Pam?

MARY. Powdering her nose – oh! Here you are Pam.

EVAN. Now where had we got to? Four diamonds, doubled. Your shout James.

JAMES. Oh – er – no bid.

(**PAM** *speaks with an acid sweetness.*)

PAM. Are you finding it difficult to keep your mind on the game, dear?

JAMES. No, of course not. What do you mean?

EVAN. What's the matter, Pam? Not feeling faint or anything are you? You look very queer.

PAM. It's just my head. I told you I had a bad head.

MARY. (*Decisively.*) Look here, I think we'd better stop. It's nearly half past seven and we've only just started this rubber. Pam's not feeling well, I can see. Come along Evan.

(*There is a pause.*)

Evan!

EVAN. All right – don't kick me. So long, you people. See you again after you come back from abroad. When are you off?

JAMES. Day after tomorrow. I am looking forward to it, I can tell you. Nowhere like *la belle France* for a holiday.

EVAN. (*Facetiously.*) Ah, but you shouldn't take the wife!

(EVAN laughs heartily.)

JAMES. Don't you believe it! It's going to be our second honeymoon!

MARY. *(Urgently.)* Come on, Evan.

JAMES. I'll see you out.

(Their voices start to recede.)

EVAN. So long, old man.

JAMES. So long.

EVAN. Bye! Mary…

PAM. *(Scornfully.)* Second honeymoon!

(MARY is heard very faintly.)

MARY. Bye! Enjoy yourselves!

(The front door bangs. JAMES returns.)

JAMES. Sorry about the head, Pam. Too much gin yesterday evening?

PAM. *(Sharply.)* Too much gin covers everything, doesn't it?

JAMES. Hullo, is something the matter? Pam darling, what have I done to make you look at me like that?

PAM. Nothing.

JAMES. Nonsense, I can see there's something. Have I said something tactless? I'll mix you a small brandy and soda.

(The chink of a glass is heard. There is a slight pause then PAM speaks dramatically.)

PAM. James, who is Fay?

(The glass drops with a crash.)

JAMES. Damn! What do you mean – Fay? What do you know about Fay?

PAM. I know that she's a woman who rings you up on a personal call – and that she wants you to come and meet her somewhere – and that she seems to know you rather well!

JAMES. So you were listening in just now?

PAM. Yes.

JAMES. My dear girl, you've got the whole thing wrong. You simply don't understand.

PAM. *(Angrily.)* You're only too right, I don't!

JAMES. It isn't the least what you think.

PAM. Isn't it?

JAMES. No dear, of course it isn't –

(He hesitates.)

As a matter of fact – well, Fay's the name of my first wife.

PAM. You told me her name was Florence.

JAMES. So it was. But I always called her Fay.

PAM. *(Ironically.)* So your former wife who has been dead for over a year, rings you up on the telephone! Most remarkable!

JAMES. Don't you see, darling, it's some wicked, stupid, practical joke! Ringing me up and pretending to be a dead woman.

(There is a pause.)

PAM. And it happened yesterday, too? And that's why you were so upset?

JAMES. Naturally. It's a particularly cruel and heartless thing to do.

PAM. But how extraordinary! Why should anyone do such a thing?

JAMES. Plenty of batty people in the world I suppose.

PAM. But James... Her voice... Did you recognise her voice? You did, didn't you? That's why you were scared as well as angry. It was Fay's voice.

JAMES. It sounded like it but, of course –

PAM. Where was it she wanted you to meet her? Some railway station or other?

JAMES. Newton Abbot.

PAM. But why Newton Abbot? And what has the time quarter past seven got to do with it?

JAMES. Because –

> *(There is pause.* **JAMES** *goes on somewhat distressed.)*

I've never cared to talk about it much. Too painful. She was killed in an accident there, you see.

PAM. At a quarter past seven?

JAMES. Well – er – yes. Oh, you might as well hear all about it. She'd been getting dizzy spells, you see. We were going back to London after a holiday we'd had on Dartmoor. We were standing on the platform waiting for the train. I went to get a paper from the bookstall. She must have felt faint and – and pitched forward on to the line just as the express came in.

PAM. Oh darling, how tragic for you.

JAMES. Yes, you can see why I never cared to talk about it.

PAM. *(Vaguely.)* Yes, yes, of course. James, yesterday – you were ringing up to find out where that personal call came from. What did they say?

JAMES. They said no personal call had been put through to me...

> *(***PAM*** draws in breath with a startled noise.)*

PAM. *(Awed.)* Suppose... It's true...

JAMES. *(Sharply.)* What?

PAM. *(Breathlessly.)* I've just been reading a book on psychical research. Really, the most extraordinary things happen... Suppose it really is Fay? Suppose her spirit is there at that railway station – waiting for you...

JAMES. *(Angrily.)* Do you think I believe that sort of silly nonsense?

PAM. Nobody would play that sort of a joke – nobody would. And you recognised her voice, darling. Queer things do happen. People who die violent deaths are earthbound, they say –

JAMES. *(Sharply.)* Who said she died a violent death?

PAM. *(Surprised.)* But she fell under the train, didn't she?

JAMES. Yes... Yes... Of course... For heaven's sake, don't go on talking about it. To forget, that's all I want – to forget! Let's talk about ourselves. Let's think how lovely it will be to get to the south of France. The mimosa will be in bloom and the Mediterranean will be – oh so blue! Why, when we get off the train –

PAM. Why don't we go by air? Much more fun.

JAMES. *(Sharply.)* No, I hate air travel.

PAM. Trains are so stuffy and take so much longer.

JAMES. *(Decisively.)* No, we're going by train. I've got the tickets and everything. That's all settled, dear.

PAM. *(Rebelliously.)* Trains! James, let's go down to this place – what is it – Newton Abbot – tomorrow. Before we go away. Let's be there, in the station, at a quarter past seven.

JAMES. *(Violently.)* Of all the idiotic suggestions! We'll do nothing of the sort. A lot of silly superstitious rubbish! It's nothing but a hoax, I tell you! And anyway, we've got other things to do tomorrow – all sorts of things. We've got an appointment with the lawyers – our two wills to sign.

PAM. *(Diverted.)* I leave you everything I've got. And you leave me everything you've got! *(Gaily.)* But I get the best of the bargain! You're really quite a rich man, aren't you, darling?

JAMES. Yes, it's annoying that my capital is tied up the way it is. But the money's there all right.

> *(He laughs boisterously.)*

You may be a rich widow one of these days!

PAM. Oh, darling – don't.

JAMES. Dearest, I was only joking. But you're right, one shouldn't joke about the things that really matter. You and I are going to have long years of happiness together.

PAM. *(Dreamily.)* Long years of happiness. I'll try and make up to you for – for all that you must have suffered.

JAMES. That's my sweet girl.

    (Fade.)

Scene Six

(A kitchen kettle is heard whistling before it is removed from the stove.)

PAM. Milk, letters, papers, bread, laundry – I think that's everything, Mrs. Lamb.

MRS. LAMB. Don't you worry, ma'am. I'll look after things for you while you're away.

PAM. Thank you, Mrs. Lamb, I'm sure you will. Well, it's after seven, you'd better be getting home.

MRS. LAMB. Wouldn't you like me to stay until Mr. Brent comes back?

PAM. No, I shall be all right. I don't expect he'll be long. You go off home.

MRS. LAMB. I'll be here first thing in the morning. And I'll bring along that packet of luggage labels you asked me to.

(The telephone rings.)

Shall I answer it, ma'am?

PAM. No, I will. Goodnight Mrs. Lamb.

(The door opens.)

MRS. LAMB. *(Faintly.)* Goodnight, ma'am.

(The front door shuts. **PAM** *lifts the telephone receiver.)*

PAM. Hullo?

MR. ENDERBY. *(Officially.)* This is Mr. Enderby of Enderby, Blenkinsop and Lucas. Can I speak to Mrs. James Brent please?

PAM. Mrs. Brent speaking.

MR. ENDERBY. Ah, good evening Mrs. Brent. You are feeling better I trust?

PAM. *(Blankly.)* Better? I'm quite all right.

MR. ENDERBY. Capital. Capital. I rang up to acknowledge the receipt of your will, duly signed and witnessed.

Your husband brought it in this afternoon. It is quite in order.

PAM. Well?

MR. ENDERBY. I am not quite clear, however, what you wish done with it? Shall it remain in our keeping or would you like it sent to your bank? I understand that you and your husband are going abroad tomorrow.

PAM. Yes, we are. Perhaps you had better send it to the bank. They have all my share certificates and things like that. Are you aware of the address?

MR. ENDERBY. Yes, yes, I have the address from your husband. Then that is all quite in order. Allow me to wish you a very pleasant trip – and no more of these dizzy fits.

PAM. Dizzy fits? What do you mean?

MR. ENDERBY. Your husband seemed quite worried about you. But I trust that they are not serious. You were very wise to rest quietly at home today and not come to my office.

PAM. But James said that it was you –

    (**PAM** *stops abruptly.*)

MR. ENDERBY. Hullo? Hullo?

PAM. Nothing.

MR. ENDERBY. Ah, I feared we had been cut off. As I was saying – now what was I saying?

PAM. You were saying that James was worried about my health. That's all nonsense. I'm perfectly well.

MR. ENDERBY. Ah, these devoted husbands! Overanxious, always overanxious. But it's a fault on the right side.

PAM. Perhaps. Well thank you, Mr. Enderby, for ringing me up.

MR. ENDERBY. Not at all. Not at all. *Bon voyage*.

PAM. Goodbye.

    (**PAM** *replaces the receiver.*)

(Bewildered.) Dizzy fits? Dizzy fits? I've never had anything of the kind.

(The telephone rings. There is a pause.)

It's just on a quarter past seven… I wonder.

(She picks up the telephone.)

Hullo? Yes?

OPERATOR. Can Mr. James Brent take a personal call from Newton Abbott?

*(**PAM** draws in a sharp breath.)*

PAM. Oh! I – he's out –

OPERATOR. Can you say when he would be available?

PAM. I – I don't quite know. This – this is Mrs. James Brent speaking. Perhaps I would do instead?

OPERATOR. Just a moment, please.

*(Silence. There is a pause. The call connects and very faint train noises are heard. **FAY**'s voice comes through much weaker and distant then before.)*

FAY. So far away… It's very difficult… Can you hear me?

PAM. This is Pamela Brent. Who are you?

FAY. I'm Fay Mortimer. I know who you are.

(A train is heard approaching.)

Don't travel with him by train.

(The train wails like a banshee.)

PAM. What? I couldn't quite hear you?

FAY. *(Distinctly.)* Don't – travel – by train – with him.

(The train enters the station. A woman's piercing scream is heard then the line goes dead.)

PAM. Hullo… Hullo… Hullo…

(The front door is heard opening.)

Hullo…

(**JAMES** *whistles a tune from the hall.*)

JAMES. Pam, what are you doing? Good Lord! You look as white as a sheet.

PAM. James, what was your first wife's name?

JAMES. *(Puzzled.)* I told you, Fay.

PAM. No, I mean her maiden name.

JAMES. Garland. Why?

PAM. It wasn't Mortimer?

(**JAMES** *falls into a panicked rage.*)

JAMES. Where did you get hold of that name? Who's been telling you things? Come on now, tell me at once.

PAM. Ouch! You're hurting me.

JAMES. *(Shouting.)* Tell me where you got hold of that name!

PAM. She said it! Through the telephone!

JAMES. *(Frightened.)* You mean… It's happened again?

PAM. Yes. She said her name was Fay Mortimer.

JAMES. Oh my God!

(There is a pause.)

(Brokenly.) I must have a drink.

(The chink of glasses is heard.)

Ah, that's better. You'd better have one too, Pam.

PAM. *(Harshly.)* I don't need one.

JAMES. *(Nervously.)* I'm sorry I lost my temper but this sort of thing – it gets a man down. Thank goodness we're going away tomorrow – right out of England.

PAM. I'm not going.

JAMES. What's that?

PAM. I'm not going.

JAMES. But why not? What's happened?

PAM. I'm not going abroad.

(There is a pause.)

I'm going down to Newton Abbot.

JAMES. You'll do nothing of the kind.

PAM. You can't stop me. If you won't come too, I shall go alone. We've got to find out what all this means...

JAMES. It's a stupid, cruel practical joke –

PAM. Don't say that again! It isn't true. Whatever it is, it isn't a joke. I think – I think – it's her...

JAMES. Her?

PAM. Fay. Come back – or never gone away. Just waiting there, where she died. Waiting for you to come.

JAMES. Stop it, Pam! Do you want to drive me mad?

PAM. You think so, too – oh yes, you do. We've got to go there and find out. If you won't come with me then I shall go by myself.

(**JAMES**' *voice fades out as he speaks.*)

JAMES. *(Sulkily.)* Of course I shall go if you're going. But I don't like it. I think you're making a great deal of unnecessary fuss about the whole thing.

Scene Seven

(Sounds of a train station.)

PORTER. Stopping train to Plymouth on the other side. Up the stairs.

WOMAN. Paddington?

PORTER. This platform. 7:15. Due in a few minutes.

WOMAN. Is there a restaurant car?

PORTER. Yes, up forwards.

MAN. Torquay?

PORTER. 7:55. Number two. Over the bridge.

*(The **STATION ANNOUNCER**'s voice booms out hoarsely.)*

STATION ANNOUNCER. The next train on number two platform is for Exeter and Paddington only. Exeter and Paddington only.

JAMES. Well Pam, I hope you're satisfied. This is Newton Abbot station. See any ghosts about?

PAM. Don't take up that sceptical attitude! We've got to be helpful.

JAMES. Helpful? To whom?

PAM. To Fay, of course.

JAMES. How you can believe this – this farrago of superstitious nonsense!

PAM. I don't believe exactly. I've just got an open mind. And don't you see? If nothing happens, we'll be free of it. You'll be free of it.

STATION ANNOUNCER. The train standing on platform number three is the stopping train for Plymouth. All stations to Plymouth.

PAM. It's nearly time now. Now you were both standing just here?

JAMES. *(Quickly.)* I wasn't. I'd gone to the bookstall to get a paper.

PAM. Yes, I know. But you left Fay here?

JAMES. Yes. She was quite all right when I left her. But she'd been having these dizzy spells –

(**PAM** *suddenly remembers.*)

PAM. James, why did you tell Mr. Enderby that I'd been having dizzy spells?

JAMES. *(Startled.)* I never – what on earth do you mean?

PAM. Why didn't we both go to his office as we arranged?

JAMES. Because I thought you had quite enough to do. Why shouldn't he send a clerk along with the papers?

PAM. But the excuse you gave him was that I had fits of dizziness?

JAMES. Nonsense. Of course I didn't. I can't imagine where he got hold of that idea.

PAM. According to him, he got it from you.

JAMES. What do you mean, according to him? You never saw the old boy.

PAM. He rang me up last night.

(**JAMES** *speaks softly to himself.*)

JAMES. Damnation.

PAM. What did you say?

JAMES. Nothing.

PAM. *(Thoughtfully.)* It would be easy to fall over on the line here if one did feel dizzy... Or if someone pushed you.

(*The sound of an approaching train is heard. The engine whistles. The* **PORTER** *shouts from some distance away.*)

PORTER. Exeter and Paddington train just coming in!

FAY. So you did come, James.

(**JAMES** *is in a terrified panic, half screaming.*)

JAMES. Fay...!

FAY. Yes, it's Fay... I've been waiting here for you. Ever since you pushed me under the train that day.

JAMES. I never meant to! It was an accident – just an accident! I didn't mean to push you. Keep away from me! Keep away!

PORTER. *(Shouting.)* Look out, sir!

> *(The train comes in.* **JAMES** *lets out a bloodcurdling scream, followed by* **PAM.** *The shrieks are quickly swallowed by the noise and whistle of the train.)*

Scene Eight

(The murmur of voices is heard against a very distant background of the station. **INSPECTOR NARRACOTT** *speaks gently, trying to rouse* **PAM**.*)*

INSPECTOR. She's all right – coming round now. Take it easy. There, like that –

PAM. Where... Where...?

INSPECTOR. You're in the stationmaster's office, Mrs. Brent. I'm Inspector Narracott. Now just you drink this. There – that's right.

PAM. James? Is he – was he –

INSPECTOR. *(Gently.)* He was killed instantly.

PAM. Oh!

INSPECTOR. This has been a great shock to you I know, Mrs. Brent, but in a way, you've been lucky. You were going away with him on a journey abroad so I've heard – and maybe you wouldn't have come back.

PAM. Not come back?

INSPECTOR. There have been three accidents that we know of. One in Northumberland and one in Wales and one here last year. In each case, the husband had mentioned previously to someone that his wife was subject to fainting or dizzy spells. And in each case, when the accident happened, the husband claimed he had gone to the bookstall to buy a paper. The names were different but it was the same man. But there was no actual evidence. And so, this lady here volunteered to help us.

*(***PAM*** gasps.)*

PAM. You! It was you who spoke to him on the platform! But you can't be Fay, you're cleverly made up, but you're not young enough.

FAY. Fay was my daughter. Our voices were always exactly alike and we looked sufficiently like each other for me to pass as her. James Mortimer had never met me.

PAM. You trapped him.

FAY. He murdered her. I always knew it, but I had to break him down. The first time I rang him up I was in London, but I pretended it was a personal call from Newton Abbot. The second time, I really did speak from Newton Abbot. The third time I rang up, he was out –

PAM. And you spoke to me instead.

FAY. *(Surprised.)* Spoke to you? No, I never spoke to you.

PAM. But you did! You warned me.

FAY. You're wrong. I just rang off.

PAM. But someone spoke to me. Someone told me not to go on a journey with him. Someone with a voice just like yours...

(**PAM** *speaks with rising hysteria.*)

Someone... Who...? Who...?

(*A last faint banshee wail from an engine is heard, dying into silence.*)

End of Play

Appendix

CHATTER BAND A
BACKGROUND OF LIGHT CHATTER

LUCY. Hullo Pam, you're looking wonderful. Marriage seems to agree with you.

PAM. Darling, it's lovely to see you. Come along and have a drink. George, you're looking more prosperous than ever.

GEORGE. Just a façade, Pam. Business is on the rocks. But you look fine.

LUCY. Don't take any notice of him, Pam, he always says business is on the rocks! But he still managed to buy me this new frock.

GEORGE. I didn't have any alternative. The first thing I saw was the bill.

PAM. Well it's lovely, anyhow. If it wasn't for James I should be quite jealous of you, darling! Now then, what are you going to drink? There's a perfectly diabolical cocktail or would you rather have sherry?

LUCY. Oh, the cocktail please. I'm going to drink myself right under the table then George will have to carry me home.

GEORGE. It won't be the first time either.

CHATTER BAND B
BACKGROUND OF MEDIUM CHATTER

JAMES. Here's your drink, Mary.

MARY. Oh, thank you, James. You really are the perfect host.

JAMES. Philip, I'm afraid you'll have to wait a bit for Pam, she's just met an old school friend.

PHILIP. Oh, I know all about old school friends! I'll just gaze at her in rapture from afar.

MARY. What's this I hear about the two of you going away?

JAMES. That's right, we're going in three days' time –

MRS. LAMB. Please, sir – please!

JAMES. *(Continues.)* How we're ever going to manage on this travel allowance, I don't know… Eh, what?

MRS. LAMB. You're wanted on the phone, sir.

JAMES. What – now? Who is it?

MRS. LAMB. It's a personal call, sir, from something Abbot.

JAMES. People will ring up at the most inconvenient moments. John, get Mona another drink. Hullo, Lois, lovely to see you. Pam's about somewhere –

MARY. What a charming man! And so handsome!

PHILIP. I wouldn't know about that, but he's certainly a very lucky man.

CHATTER BAND C
BACKGROUND OF LIGHT CHATTER

JOHNNIE. I can't see anything to prevent Surrey winning the championship again this year. Just look at their bowlers.

DAVID. *(Laughing.)* I say, these crisps are good. What's that? Surrey? Don't you believe it, old boy. Yorkshire are going to win the championship.

JOHNNIE. But look, Surrey have got Bedser, Lock and Laker, all test match bowlers. Then there's Loader, who's a future England player, quite apart from Surridge and Eric Bedser.

DAVID. Have a crisp, old boy, and curb your youthful enthusiasm.

CHATTER BAND D
BACKGROUND OF MEDIUM CHATTER

PAM. Mary, Evan, how nice of you to come.

EVAN. Hello Pam, you're looking more beautiful than ever.

MARY. Darling, I haven't seen you for ages. Can't we get into a corner somewhere – I want to hear all about you and James.

CHATTER BAND E
BACKGROUND OF EXUBERANT CHATTER

EVAN. Hullo James, there you are. You're a very elusive host.

JAMES. Hullo Evan, not seen you for ages. I hear you're coming in to bridge tomorrow? Good show...

EVAN. That's right, old boy. We're going to take all your money off you before you go on your holiday.

JAMES. Come on you, let's have another drink.

Yellow Iris

CHARACTERS

HERCULE POIROT
PAULINE WEATHERBY
SEÑORA LOLA VALDEZ
BARTON RUSSELL
ANTHONY CHAPPELL
STEPHEN CARTER
WAITER
CLOAKROOM ATTENDANT
COMPÉRE

YELLOW IRIS was first performed on the BBC National Programme on Tuesday 2 November 1937. The original broadcast was featured with music composed by Michael Sayer and lyrics by Christopher Hassall. The cast was as follows:

HERCULE POIROT	Anthony Holles
PAULINE WEATHERBY	Evelyn Neilson
SEÑORA LOLA VALDEZ	Martita Hunt
BARTON RUSSELL	Sydney Keith
ANTHONY CHAPPELL	Frank Drew
STEPHEN CARTER	Peter Scott
WAITER	Dino Galvani
CLOAKROOM ATTENDANT	Audrey Cameron
COMPÉRE	Bernard Jukes

Scene One

(The restaurant of the hotel Jardin des Cygnes. Mixed restaurant chatter is heard.)

PAULINE. *(Urgently.)* Waiter! Waiter!

WAITER. Mademoiselle?

PAULINE. Where can I telephone? It's desperately urgent.

WAITER. The telephone, mam'selle, is in there.

PAULINE. Thank you.

(The restaurant chatter fades.)

Scene Two

(The hotel lobby. The porter's bell from the front desk is heard. The **CLOAKROOM ATTENDANT** *speaks efficiently as* **SEÑORA LOLA VALDEZ** *arrives.)*

ATTENDANT. Good evening, madam. Can I take your cloak?

LOLA. Yes, please.

ATTENDANT. Thank you, madam.

LOLA. Tell me, the telephone – where is it?

ATTENDANT. The telephone, madam? Just outside this cloakroom, on your right, madam.

LOLA. Ah yes. Thank you. *(Quietly.)* Is it private? I have a very important personal message to give. I would not like anyone to –

ATTENDANT. Quite private, madam. On your right as you go out.

LOLA. Oh, thank you.

(Fade.)

Scene Three

(The study of **HERCULE POIROT**. *The telephone rings.)*

POIROT. Hélas! Never is there peace.

(He calls.)

Jules! Jules! Le téléphone!

(There is no reply. The telephone continues to ring.)

Zut alors!

(He lifts the receiver.)

Hallo!

*(***PAULINE** *speaks, disguising her voice.)*

PAULINE. *(Urgently.)* Is that Monsieur Hercule Poirot? Is that Hercule Poirot?

POIROT. Hercule Poirot speaks!

PAULINE. Monsieur Poirot, can you come at once – at once? I'm in great danger, I know it!

POIROT. Who are you? From where are you speaking?

*(***PAULINE** *sounds more distant.)*

PAULINE. At once… It may be life or death! The Jardin des Cygnes…at once…table with yellow irises –

(The line goes dead.)

POIROT. Hallo! Hallo!

(He rattles the receiver.)

Hallo! *(Quietly.)* The Jardin des Cygnes, hein? There is something here very curious.

(Fade.)

Scene Four

(Restaurant at Jardin des Cygnes. Mixed restaurant chatter and music.)

["YOU'RE GOOD FOR MY BAD HABITS"]

CHORUS

> YOU'RE GOOD FOR MY BAD HABITS,
> I CAN'T REMEMBER NOW
> THE WAY TO SAY, "OH! BLIMEY!"
> TRY ME – NO KIDDIN' –
> YOU'RE GOOD FOR MY BAD HABITS,
> YOU'VE DONE THE TRICK SOMEHOW,
> AND ALL WITHOUT A SINGLE ROW.
> FOR YEARS I'VE WAITED
> FOR SOMEONE THAT LOVED ME YET HATED
> ME BITING MY NAILS.
> YOU GAVE ME SOMETHING TO CARE FOR,
> AND THEREFORE
> I WENT BACK ON THE RAILS.
> YOU'RE GOOD FOR MY BAD HABITS,
> IF I COULD MARRY YOU,
> YOU'D FIND THAT I COULD DO GOOD TOO.

VERSE

> SOME PEOPLE LIVE IN A CHRONIC HURRY,
> NOTHING BUT WORRY
> ALL THE DAY THROUGH
> BUT LIFE WILL MOVE IN A NEW DIRECTION
> WHEN THERE'S AFFECTION
> TO GUIDE YOU.

(The CHORUS reprises over the following dialogue.)

WAITER. Buona sera, Monsieur Poirot. Welcome to the Jardin des Cygnes. You desire a table, yes?

POIROT. No, no, my good Luigi. I seek here for some friends – perhaps they are not here yet.

WAITER. It is a big party?

POIROT. Non – non. Ah, let me see, that table in the corner with the yellow irises!

WAITER. Yes?

POIROT. A little question, if it is not indiscreet. On all the other tables there are tulips – pink tulips. Why on that one table have you yellow irises?

WAITER. A command, monsieur – a special order. No doubt to please one of the ladies.

POIROT. But of course. And the table is…?

WAITER. Mr. Barton Russell's table – an American. Rich, oh là là, so rich!

POIROT. Aha, and one must study the whims of the ladies, must one not, my good Luigi?

WAITER. Monsieur has said it.

(Light applause is heard at the end of the number.)

POIROT. But tiens, I see at the table an acquaintance of mine. I must go and speak to him!

(There is a pause.)

Bon soir! Bon soir! Is it not my friend Anthony Chappell?

CHAPPELL. By all that's wonderful, Poirot, the police hound. Come and sit down. Let us discourse of crime. Let us go further and drink to crime!

POIROT. Thank you, mon cher Anthony.

(An instrumental version of "You Live In My Heart" underscores the restaurant chatter.)

CHAPPELL. There's a glass there!

POIROT. A little only…

CHAPPELL. Now tell me what you're doing here. There isn't a dead body in the place – positively not a single one!

POIROT. You seem very gay, mon cher?

CHAPPELL. Gay? I'm steeped in misery, wallowing in gloom. *(Confidentially.)* You hear this tune they're playing?

POIROT. Yes?

CHAPPELL. You recognise it?

POIROT. Something perhaps to do with your baby having left you?

CHAPPELL. Not a bad guess, but wrong for once. "You Live In My Heart" – that's what it's called!

POIROT. Aha!

CHAPPELL. *(Mournfully.)* My favourite tune – my favourite restaurant and my favourite band. And my favourite girl is here and she's dancing it with someone else!

POIROT. Hence the melancholy?

CHAPPELL. Exactly. Pauline and I, you see, have had what the vulgar call "words." That's to say, she's had ninety-five out of every one hundred. My five are, "But darling, I can explain!" Then she starts in again with her ninety-five and we get no further. I think I shall poison myself!

POIROT. Pauline?

CHAPPELL. Pauline Weatherby. Barton Russell's sister-in-law. Young, lovely, disgustingly rich. This is Barton's party. D'you know him?

POIROT. Non, I have still the pleasure. Who else is at this party?

CHAPPELL. You'll meet 'em in a minute. Forgive me, Monsieur Poirot, but that girl's going to sing.

POIROT. And this being your favourite tune – perhaps the lyric has a special message?

CHAPPELL. Perhaps!

["YOU LIVE IN MY HEART"]

I HAD NO CHOICE BUT TO ADORE YOU
SOON AS I SAW YOU.
UNDER THE MOON
THIS NEW ROMANCE
HAS ONLY JUST STARTED,
WHY MUST WE BE PARTED
SO SOON?
YOU LIVE IN MY HEART,

AND YOU'RE A PART OF ALL THE LOVELINESS
I SEE.
YOU LIVE IN MY DREAMS,
EVEN THE SCHEMES
I MAKE ARE FASHIONED FOR YOU ONLY.
YOU LIVE IN MY HEART,
NO MATTER HOW THE WAVES OF OCEAN ROLL BETWEEN.
RIGHT – RIGHT FROM THE START,
I'VE ALWAYS HELD YOU CLOSE FOR YOU TO LIVE
IN MY HEART.

(Warm applause and mixed chatter is heard.)

(Sighing.) Ah, well!

POIROT. A very "affecting" lyric, mon vieux – but before it, you were telling me who was at this party apart from the charming Miss Weatherby.

CHAPPELL. Oh yes, of course. Well, there's Lola Valdez – you know, the South American dancer in the metropole show. Stephen Carter, he's in the diplomatic – very hush, hush – known as Silent Stephen – he's… Hullo, here they come. Here's somebody I want you to meet –

(There is a pause.)

Barton Russell – Monsieur Hercule Poirot.

RUSSELL. What, is this the great Monsieur Poirot? I'm very glad to meet you, sir. Let me introduce Señora Valdez.

VALDEZ. How do you do?

POIROT. Enchanté, mademoiselle!

RUSSELL. And Miss Weatherby.

POIROT. Enchanté, mademoiselle!

PAULINE. How do you do!

RUSSELL. Won't you sit down and join us? That is unless…

CHAPPELL. He's got an appointment with a body, I believe. Or is it an absconding financier?

POIROT. Ah, my friend, do you think I am never off duty? May I not for once seek only to amuse myself?

CHAPPELL. Perhaps you've got an appointment with Carter here? The latest from Geneva! Stolen plans must be found or war declared tomorrow!

PAULINE. *(Cuttingly.)* Must you be so completely idiotic, Tony?

CHAPPELL. Sorry, Pauline.

POIROT. How severe you are, mademoiselle!

PAULINE. I hate people who play the fool all the time.

POIROT. Ah, then I must converse only of serious matters!

PAULINE. Oh no, Monsieur Poirot, I didn't mean you!

POIROT. Ah, bon.

PAULINE. Are you really a kind of Sherlock Holmes and do wonderful deductions?

POIROT. Ah, the deductions – they are not so easy in real life. But shall I try?

PAULINE. Yes, do!

POIROT. Now then, I deduce – that yellow irises are your favourite flowers?

PAULINE. Quite wrong, Monsieur Poirot. Lily of the Valley or roses!

POIROT. *(Sighs.)* A failure. Never mind, I will try once more. This evening, not very long ago, you telehphoned to someone.

PAULINE. Quite right!

POIROT. It was not long after you arrived here?

PAULINE. Right again. I telephoned the minute I got inside doors.

POIROT. Ah, that is not so good. You telephoned *before* you came to this table?

PAULINE. Yes.

POIROT. Decidedly very bad.

PAULINE. Oh no, I think it was very clever of you. How did you know I had telephoned?

POIROT. That, mademoiselle, is a great detective's secret. And the person to whom you telephoned – does his name begin with a P – or perhaps with an H?

PAULINE. *(Laughs.)* Quite wrong. I telephoned to my maid to post some frightfully important letters that I'd never sent off. Her name's Louise.

(Instrumental of "Your Heart Was In My Hands" begins to play.)

POIROT. I am confused – quite confused. Can it be that I need practice? Ah, what charming music. La Valse. Do you not dance, mam'selle?

CHAPPELL. Yes, what about it, Pauline?

PAULINE. I don't think I want to dance again so soon, Tony.

CHAPPELL. Isn't that too bad?

POIROT. Señora Valdez, I would not dare to ask you to dance with me. I am too much of the antique.

VALDEZ. Ah, it is nonsense that you talk there! You are still young. Your hair, it is still black!

(Polite laughter is heard from the group.)

RUSSELL. Pauline, as your brother-in-law, I'm just going to force you on to the floor! This one's a waltz and a waltz is about the only dance I really can do.

PAULINE. Why, of course, Barton. We'll take the floor right away.

RUSSELL. Good girl Pauline, that's swell of you.

PAULINE. Come along then, I'm waiting.

(The restaurant chatter fades as the vocal begins.)

["YOUR HEART WAS IN MY HANDS"]

CAN'T WE RECAPTURE
THE RAPTURE
THAT MADE ALL THE WORLD SEEM GAY?
SURELY TOMORROW
OUR SORROW
WILL FADE ALL AWAY – DWINDLE AWAY.

YOUR HEART WAS IN MY HANDS,
AND YET I LET YOU GO.
WHAT HAVE WE TO SHOW
FOR ALL THE LOVE WE CHERISHED?
YOUR HEART WAS IN MY HANDS
BUT I WAS IN A DREAM,
LIFE APPEARED TO FLOW
JUST LIKE A STREAM.
I KNEW NOT A SAD MORNING
WAS SOON GOING TO BREAK
AND WHEN I WAS AWAKE
REVEAL MY MISTAKE.
YOUR HEART WAS IN MY HANDS
AND MINE HAS VANISHED TOO
MINE SHALL EVER STAY WITH YOU.

> *(An orchestral reprise begins. Mixed chatter is heard.)*

CHAPPELL. Pretty creature Pauline is – especially when she's dancing, eh Carter?

> *(There is a pause.)*

I say, talkative little fellow, aren't you, Carter? Help to make a party go with your merry chatter, eh what?

CARTER. Really, Chappell, I don't know what you mean.

CHAPPELL. Oh, you don't – don't you?

CARTER. My dear fellow.

CHAPPELL. Well, drink man, drink, if you won't talk!

CARTER. No thanks.

CHAPPELL. Then I will.

CARTER. *(Coldly.)* Excuse me, must just speak to a fellow I know over there. Fellow I was at school with.

> *(There is a pause.* **CHAPPELL** *speaks almost to himself.)*

CHAPPELL. Somebody ought to have drowned him at birth.

POIROT. It is not my affair, but were you not a little harsh, mon vieux!

VALDEZ. Poor Mister Carter looks very hurt!

CHAPPELL. Oh, Silent Stephen can look after himself. Does him good.

POIROT. I wonder, may I ask, what are the favourite flowers of mademoiselle?

VALDEZ. *(Archly.)* Ah now, why is it you want to know?

POIROT. Mademoiselle, if I send flowers to a lady, I am particular that they should be flowers she likes.

VALDEZ. That is very charming of you, Monsieur Poirot. I will tell you, I adore the big dark red carnations or the dark red roses.

POIROT. Superb – yes, superb! You do not, then, like yellow flowers – yellow irises?

VALDEZ. Yellow flowers? No, they do not accord with my temperament.

POIROT. How wise. Tell me, mademoiselle, did you ring up a friend tonight, since you arrived here?

VALDEZ. I? Ring up a friend? No, what a curious question.

POIROT. Ah, but I, I am a very curious man.

(Light applause is heard as the number ends.)

VALDEZ. I'm sure you are. And a very dangerous man.

POIROT. No, no, not dangerous – say, a man who may be *useful* in danger!

VALDEZ. *(Giggles.)* No, no. You are dangerous.

POIROT. *(Sighs.)* I see that you do not understand. All this is very strange.

(Instrumental of "There's Danger in the Tango Band" begins.)

CHAPPELL. Lola, what about a spot of swoop and dip? Come along.

VALDEZ. I will come, yes. Since Monsieur Poirot is not brave enough!

CHAPPELL. He has no time for frivolous things like dancing. You can meditate on the crime to be committed, old boy!

POIROT. It is profound what you say there. Yes, it is profound...

> *(The restaurant chatter fades as the vocal begins.)*

["THERE'S DANGER IN THE TANGO BAND"]

I KNOW A LADY SO EXOTIC,
SHE'D MAKE A DUMMY FEEL EROTIC,
SHE'S JUST ABOUT AS 'LURING AS CAN BE!
YOU'LL SOON BE SO ENTHUSIASTIC
AND IN THE MOOD FOR SOMETHING DRASTIC,
JUST LISTEN TO ME, WAIT TILL YOU SEE.

THERE'S A WOMAN IN THE TANGO BAND,
SHE'S THE TERROR OF THE TANGO BAND!
LOOK AT THE RINGS TOO,
GIVEN BY KINGS WHO
WANTED TO WIN HER HAND!
THERE'S DANGER IN THE TANGO BAND!
WHEN SHE PLAYS UPON HER SOFT GUITAR,
SHE'D MAKE MILLIONS AS A MOVIE STAR.
SUCH A TEMPTATION, SUCH A SENSATION,
YOU DON'T KNOW WHERE YOU ARE.

THERE'S DANGER IN HER SOFT GUITAR.
SURELY SHE'S PERFECTION,
THAT BROWN COMPLEXION,
THAT JET-BLACK HAIR.
SHE WILL SMILE SO SWEETLY,
YOU'RE LOST COMPLETELY,
BEWARE! FOR
THERE'S A WOMAN IN THE TANGO BAND,
SHE'S THE TERROR OF THE TANGO BAND.
O SO ROMANTIC,
SHE'LL DRIVE YOU FRANTIC,
SO NOW YOU UNDERSTAND.
THERE'S DANGER IN THE TANGO BAND.

(Light laughter and applause are heard. An orchestral reprise begins and mixed chatter is heard.)

POIROT. Luigi! Luigi!

WAITER. Monsieur called?

POIROT. Mon vieux, I need some information.

WAITER. Always at your service, monsieur.

POIROT. I desire to know how many of these people at this table here have used the telephone tonight?

WAITER. I can tell you, monsieur. The young lady, the one in white, she telephoned at once when she got here. Then she went to leave her cloak, and while she was doing that, the other young lady came out of the cloakroom and went into the telephone box.

POIROT. So the señora did telephone! Was that *before* she came into the restaurant?

WAITER. Yes, monsieur.

POIROT. All this, Luigi, gives me furiously to think!

WAITER. Indeed, monsieur?

POIROT. Yes, I think, Luigi, that tonight of all nights, I must have my wits about me! Something is going to happen, Luigi, and I am not at all sure what it is.

WAITER. Anything I can do, monsieur?

POIROT. Thank you, Luigi. Leave me for a moment. Here is Mr. Carter coming back!

WAITER. Very good, monsieur!

(There is a slight pause.)

POIROT. Hélas! We are still deserted, Mr. Carter.

CARTER. Oh – er – quite.

POIROT. You know Mr. Barton Russell well?

CARTER. Yes, known him quite a good while.

POIROT. His sister-in-law, little Miss Weatherby, is very charming.

CARTER. Yes, pretty girl.

POIROT. You know her well, too?

CARTER. Quite.

POIROT. Oh quite, quite.

(Light applause is heard as the number ends. Mixed chatter is heard as guests return from the dance floor.)

RUSSELL. I hope we haven't left you too long, Monsieur Poirot?

POIROT. But no. I find much entertainment here.

RUSSELL. Ah, good. I'm glad of that. Come along, Lola. I want everyone here. I guess I've a little speech to make. Sit down, Pauline – you, too, Tony. That's right. Say, waiter, where's that bottle of champagne?

WAITER. Here sir, at once, sir.

RUSSELL. See here, folks, I'm going to ask you to drink a toast. To tell you the truth, there's an idea back of this little party tonight. As you know, I'd ordered a table for six. There were only five of us. That gave us an empty place. Then, by a very strange coincidence, Monsieur Hercule Poirot happened to pass by and I asked him to join our party. You don't know yet what an apt coincidence that was. You see that empty seat tonight represents a lady – the lady in whose memory this party is being given. This party, ladies and gentlemen, is being held in memory of my dear wife – Iris – who died exactly four years ago on this very date.

(There is a slight gasp from the guests.)

I'll ask you to drink to her memory. Iris!

POIROT. Iris?

ALL. Iris – Iris... The flowers, don't you see? Yellow irises – etc., etc.

RUSSELL. It may seem odd to you all that I should celebrate the anniversary of a death in this way – by a supper party in a fashionable restaurant. But I have a reason, yes, I have a reason. For Monsieur Poirot's benefit, I'll explain.

PAULINE. But Barton –

RUSSELL. Please Pauline! Four years ago tonight, Monsieur Poirot, there was a supper party held at a club not unlike this in New York. At it were my wife and myself, Mr. Stephen Carter, who was attached to the embassy in Washington, Mr. Anthony Chappell, who had been a guest in our house for some weeks, and Señora Valdez, who was at that time enchanting New York City with her dancing. And, of course, my sister-in-law had unexpectedly come to stay. You remember, Pauline?

PAULINE. The weather had stopped me sailing home. I remember, yes.

RUSSELL. Monsieur Poirot, on that night a tragedy happened. There was a roll of drums and the cabaret started. The lights went down – all but a spot light in the middle of the floor. When the lights went up again, my wife was seen to have fallen forward on the table. She was dead – stone dead. There was potassium cyanide found in the dregs of her wine glass, and the remains of the packet were discovered in her handbag.

POIROT. She had committed suicide?

RUSSELL. That was the accepted verdict. It broke me, Monsieur Poirot. There was, perhaps, a possible reason for such an action – the police thought so. I accepted their decision.

(He beats his fist on table.)

But I was not satisfied. No, for four years I've been thinking and brooding and I'm not satisfied! I don't believe Iris killed herself. I believe, Monsieur Poirot, that she was murdered by one of those people at the table.

CHAPPELL. Look here, sir –

RUSSELL. Be quiet, Tony, I haven't finished. One of them did it, I'm sure of that now. Someone who, under cover of the darkness, slipped the half emptied packet of cyanide into her handbag. I think I know which of them it was. I mean to know the truth –

VALDEZ. You are mad – crazy – who would have harmed her? No, you are mad. Me, I will not stay –

POIROT. Gently, mademoiselle, gently.

> *(A roll of drums and cymbals are heard.* **RUSSELL** *speaks over the* **COMPERE** *who is heard in the background.)*

RUSSELL. The cabaret. Afterwards we will go on with this. Stay where you are, all of you. I've got to go and speak to the dance band leader. Little arrangement I've made with him.

COMPERE. Ladies and gentlemen. We now come to this evening's cabaret, in which we present first the celebrated torch singer, Inga Anderson in a number which she has brought with her from New York, where she sang it with great success. Here she is, ladies and gentlemen – Inga Anderson direct from New York – to sing you "Interrupted Rhythm!"

CARTER. Extraordinary business – man's mad.

VALDEZ. He is crazy, yes.

CHAPPELL. For two pins I'd clear out. I think we all ought to!

PAULINE. No!

> *(****PAULINE*** *speaks to herself.)*

Oh dear – oh dear –

POIROT. What is it, mademoiselle?

PAULINE. *(Whispers.)* It's horrible! It's just like it was that night.

EVERYONE. Shh! Shh!

POIROT. A little word in your ear. All will be well.

> *(Instrumental of "Interrupted Rhythm" begins to play.)*

VALDEZ. My God, listen!

POIROT. What is it, señora?

VALDEZ. It's the same tune – the same song that they played that night in New York. Barton Russell must have fixed it. I do not like this.

POIROT. Courage – courage.

["INTERRUPTED RHYTHM"]

IN THIS CIVILISATION, FULL OF MAD SYNCOPATION,
I GROW SICK OF THE DIN WE'RE MAKIN'.
THERE'S NO PLACE YOU CAN FLY TO,
IT'S NO GOOD IF YOU TRY TO,
EVERY NERVE IN YOUR BODY
IS SHAKIN' – BREAKIN',
WHETHER YOU'RE SLEEPIN' OR WAKIN'.

ALL ALONG THE MIDNIGHT HIGHWAY,
UNDERNEATH THE TRAFFIC'S ROAR,
THO' YOU MAY FEAR IT,
YOU'RE CERTAIN TO HEAR IT
INTERRUPTED RHYTHM DRUMMIN' LIKE WAR.
EVEN IN THE DARKENED BEDROOM,
WHERE IT'S NEVER BEEN BEFORE.
DRONIN' AND DRUMMIN', YOU'LL SOON HEAR IT COMIN'
INTERRUPTED RHYTHM IS AT THE DOOR.
WHILE I'M SINUOUSLY SWAYING, THROUGH THE LIMELIGHT,
GAILY DRESSED,
THERE'S A HEART IN ME IS PRAYING FOR THE SHANTY,
OUT WEST, WHERE THERE IS REST.
MILLIONS OF CRAZY PEOPLE JOGGIN' ON THE JAZZ BAND FLOOR.
JUST AS I'M SPEAKIN' ARE EVERYWHERE SHRIEKIN',
INTERRUPTED RHYTHM, GIVE US SOME MORE!

(A burst of applause is heard, as the song ends.)

WAITER. Champagne, miss? Champagne, sir?
CHAPPELL. She's great, that girl! Lord, what a voice!
VALDEZ. *(Screaming.)* Look! Look!
CHAPPELL. Pauline! Darling!
VALDEZ. She's dead! Just like Iris – like Iris in New York!
POIROT. Quickly there. Draw the curtain, nobody must see!
RUSSELL. But it's impossible, she can't be dead!

POIROT. Yes, she is dead – la pauvre petite. And I, sitting by her! Ah! But this time the murderer shall not escape!

RUSSELL. Just like Iris! She saw something – Pauline saw something that night only she wasn't sure – she told me she wasn't sure! We must get the police! Oh God, my poor Pauline!

POIROT. No, no, we can do without the police! Where is her glass? Yes, I can smell the cyanide. A smell of bitter almonds. The same method, the same poison. Let us look in her handbag.

RUSSELL. You don't believe this is suicide, too? Not on your life.

POIROT. Wait. No, there is nothing here. The lights went up, you see, too quickly – the murderer had not time. Therefore, the poison is still on him.

CARTER. Or her.

VALDEZ. What do you mean – what do you say? That I kill her! It is not true – not true! Why should I do such a thing!

POIROT. Really, Mr. Carter!

CARTER. You had rather a fancy for Barton Russell yourself in New York. That's the gossip I heard. Argentine beauties are notoriously jealous.

VALDEZ. That is a pack of lies! And I do not come from the Argentine. I come from Peru. Ah, I spit upon you – I –

(She lapses into Spanish in her anger.)

POIROT. I demand silence. It is for me to speak.

RUSSELL. Everyone must be searched.

POIROT. *(Calmly.)* Non, non, it is not necessary.

RUSSELL. What d'you mean, not necessary?

POIROT. I, Hercule Poirot, know. I see with the eyes of the mind. And I will speak! Monsieur Carter, will you show us the packet in your breast pocket?

CARTER. There's nothing in my pocket. What the hell –

POIROT. Tony, my good friend, if you will be so obliging.

CARTER. Damn you – take your hands away!

CHAPPELL. There you are, Poirot. Just as you said – a packet!

CARTER. It's a damned lie!

POIROT. Cyanide of potassium. The case is complete.

RUSSELL. Carter! I always thought so. Iris was in love with you. She wanted to go away with you. You didn't want a scandal for the sake of your precious career, so you poisoned her. You'll hang for this, you dirty dog.

POIROT. Silence! This is not finished yet. I, Hercule Poirot, have something to say. My friend here, Tony Chappell, he says to me when I arrive, that I have come in search of crime. That, it is partly true. There was crime in my mind – but it was to prevent a crime that I came. And I have prevented it. The murderer, he planned well – but Hercule Poirot he was one move ahead. He had to think fast, and to whisper quickly in mademoiselle's ear when the lights went down. She is very quick and clever, Mademoiselle Pauline, she played her part well. Mademoiselle, will you be so kind as to show us that you are not dead after all?

(**PAULINE** *laughs shakily.*)

PAULINE. Resurrection of Pauline.

(*Everybody gasps.*)

CHAPPELL. Pauline – darling!

PAULINE. Tony!

CHAPPELL. My sweet!

PAULINE. Angel!

RUSSELL. I – I don't understand...

POIROT. I will help you to understand, Mr. Barton Russell. Your plan has miscarried.

RUSSELL. My plan?

POIROT. Yes, your plan. Who was the only man who had an alibi during the darkness? The man who left the table. You, Mr. Barton Russell. But you returned to it under cover of the darkness, circling round it, with a champagne bottle, filling up glasses, putting cyanide in Pauline's glass and dropping the half empty packet in Carter's pocket as you bent over him to remove a glass. Oh yes, it is easy to play the part of a waiter in darkness when the attention of everyone is elsewhere. That was the real reason for your party tonight. The safest place to commit a murder is in the middle of a crowd.

RUSSELL. What the – why the hell should I want to kill Pauline?

POIROT. It might be, perhaps, a question of money. Your wife left you guardian to her sister. You mentioned that fact tonight. Pauline is twenty. At twenty-one, or on her marriage, you would have to render an account of your stewardship. I suggest that you could not do that. You have speculated with it. I do not know, Mr. Barton Russell, whether you killed your wife in the same way, or whether her suicide suggested the idea of this crime to you, but I do know that tonight you have been guilty of attempted murder. It rests with Miss Pauline whether you are prosecuted for that.

PAULINE. No. He can get out of my sight and out of this country. I don't want another scandal.

POIROT. You had better go quickly, Mr. Barton Russell, and I advise you to be careful in future.

RUSSELL. To hell with you, you interfering little Belgian jackanapes.

POIROT. *(Threateningly.)* Goodbye, Mr. Russell.

RUSSELL. Bah!

(There is a pause.)

POIROT. And that, my friends, is that!

PAULINE. Monsieur Poirot, you've been wonderful.

POIROT. You, mademoiselle, you have been the marvellous one. To pour away the champagne, to act the dead body so prettily. It was you who telephoned me, was it not?

PAULINE. Yes.

POIROT. Why?

PAULINE. I don't know. I was worried and frightened, without knowing quite why I was frightened. Barton told me he was having this party to commemorate Iris' death. I realised he had some scheme on, but he wouldn't tell me what it was. He looked so – so queer and so excited that I felt something terrible might happen. Only, of course, I never dreamt that he meant to – to get rid of me.

POIROT. And so, mademoiselle?

PAULINE. I'd heard Tony talking about you. I thought if I could only get you here perhaps it would stop anything happening. I thought that being a – a foreigner, if I rang up and pretended to be in danger and – and made it sound mysterious –

POIROT. You thought the melodrama, it would attract me? That is what puzzled me – the message itself – definitely it was what you call "bogus." It did not ring true. But the fear in the voice – that was real. Then I came and you denied, very categorically, having sent me a message.

PAULINE. I had to. Besides, I didn't want you to know it was me.

POIROT. Ah. I was fairly sure of that! Not at first. But I soon realised that the only two people who could know about the yellow irises on the table were you or Mr. Barton Russell.

PAULINE. Yes, I heard him ordering them to be put on the table. That, and his ordering a table for six, when I knew only five were coming, made me suspect.

POIROT. What did you suspect, mademoiselle?

PAULINE. I was afraid of something happening to – Mr. Carter.

POIROT. Mr. Carter – so?

CARTER. Er – hm – I have to – er – thank you, Monsieur Poirot. I owe you a great deal. You'll excuse me, I'm sure, if I leave you. Tonight's happenings have been – rather upsetting. Goodnight. Goodnight.

> *(There is a pause.)*

PAULINE. *(Violently.)* I hate him. I've always thought it was because of him that Iris killed herself. Or perhaps, Barton killed her. Oh it's all so hateful!

POIROT. Forget, mademoiselle.

> *(The orchestra starts a slow foxtrot.)*

Forget. Let the past go. Think only of the present.

PAULINE. Yes – you're right.

POIROT. Señora Valdez, as the evening advances I become more brave. If you would dance with me now –

VALDEZ. Oh yes, indeed. You are – you are the cat's whiskers, Monsieur Poirot. I insist on dancing with you. After tonight's happening I need the protection of such a man as you!

POIROT. You are too kind, señora. To dance with Señora Lola Valdez is indeed an honour.

VALDEZ. *(Laughing.)* Oh, Monsieur Poirot, you flatterer. Ha! Ha! Ha!

CHAPPELL. Pauline – Pauline.

PAULINE. Yes, Tony?

CHAPPELL. Darling.

PAULINE. Oh, Tony, I've been such a nasty, spiteful, spitfiring little cat to you all day. Can you ever forgive me?

CHAPPELL. Angel! This is our tune again. Let's dance.

PAULINE. Of course, my sweet.

> *(The restaurant chatter fades with a vocal refrain of "You Live In My Heart.")*

["YOU LIVE IN MY HEART"]

SINGER.
YOU LIVE IN MY HEART,
AND YOU'RE A PART OF ALL THE LOVELINESS I SEE.

TOGETHER.
>YOU LIVE IN MY DREAMS,
>EVEN THE SCHEMES
>I MAKE ARE FASHIONED FOR YOU ONLY.
>YOU LIVE IN MY HEART,
>NO MATTER HOW THE WAVES OF OCEAN ROLL BETWEEN.

SINGER.
>RIGHT, RIGHT FROM THE START,
>I'VE ALWAYS HELD YOU CLOSE
>FOR YOU LIVE IN MY HEART.

TOGETHER.
>YOU EVER LIVE IN MY HEART.

End of Play

Butter in a Lordly Dish

CHARACTERS

SIR LUKE ENDERBY K.C.
LADY ENDERBY
JULIA KEENE
SUSAN WARREN
MRS. PETTER
FLORRIE PETTER
HAYWARD
A PORTER

BUTTER IN A LORDLY DISH was first performed on the BBC Radio Light Programme on Tuesday 13 January 1948 and produced by Martyn C. Webster. The cast was as follows:

SIR LUKE ENDERBY K.C. . . . . Richard Williams
LADY ENDERBY . . . . Lydia Sherwood
JULIA KEENE . . . . Rita Vale
SUSAN WARREN . . . . .Thea Wells
MRS. PETTER . . . . Dora Gregory
FLORRIE PETTER . . . . .Jill Nyasa
HAYWARD . . . . .Janet Morrison
A PORTER. . . . . David Kossoff

Scene One

*(The confused noises of a London street are heard. "Star," "Standard," "The News." A distant door opens and bangs and street noise fade. **FLORRIE** calls in a clear cockney accent.)*

FLORRIE. Hi, Mums?

MRS. PETTER. That you, Florrie?

FLORRIE. Yes.

(A door opens.)

MRS. PETTER. Hello dear.

FLORRIE. *(Sniffs.)* Is my nose telling me there's somethin' good for tea?

MRS. PETTER. Fish and chips.

FLORRIE. H'm, good.

(The door closes.)

Oh drat! What's all these suitcases doing here? Doesn't half clutter the place up.

MRS. PETTER. It's Mrs. Keene's things.

FLORRIE. Oh, the lodger. She going away?

MRS. PETTER. Yes, but she's not going to take these with her – only one small case.

FLORRIE. Why?

MRS. PETTER. Because she's not certain yet where she'll be. She'll let us know where she wants all this sent.

FLORRIE. Seems peculiar to me – going away and not knowing where she's going.

MRS. PETTER. What do you mean?

FLORRIE. I'll bet she's off for the weekend with someone.

MRS. PETTER. Now don't talk like that. It's not nice.

FLORRIE. All right, but if you ask me, there's something fishy about our Mrs. Keene.

MRS. PETTER. Now stop it, Florrie. She's a very nice lady. Always speaks so pleasant.

FLORRIE. That's the kind that gets things from shops without paying for them. Confidence tricksters, they call them. Mind she pays you before she waltzes off.

MRS. PETTER. She has paid me, right up to tomorrow and a bit over for leaving the cases and sending them on. So you ought to be ashamed of yourself for being so suspicious.

FLORRIE. All right – but I know what I know.

MRS. PETTER. What do you know?

FLORRIE. Well, it was last week. I was going along from Park Lane into Berkeley Square and there was a party on at one of those big houses, you know, cocktails and sherry and all that.

MRS. PETTER. Well!

FLORRIE. Well, who should I see coming out with a tall, handsome man but our Mrs. Keene. Dressed up to the nines, fox furs and one of those flyaway black velvet hats. I will say she looked a treat, but it's odd, you'll admit.

MRS. PETTER. What?

FLORRIE. Going to swell society houses all dressed up and lodging here with us just off the Pimlico Road. It doesn't fit, somehow.

MRS. PETTER. And I suppose you've got some far-fetched notion to account for it.

FLORRIE. If you ask me, she's in with one of those gangs of society burglars.

MRS. PETTER. The nonsense you talk.

FLORRIE. She goes along to places and finds out where the stuff is kept, and when the house is likely to be empty, and passes the word on to the gang.

MRS. PETTER. And if you ask me, you go too much to the pictures! Gangs, indeed!

FLORRIE. Well, gangs aren't only on at the pictures. You read about them in the newspapers, too.

MRS. PETTER. Nonsense.

FLORRIE. Come off it, Mum, you like a nice little bit of crime yourself.

MRS. PETTER. Talking of crime, is that an evening paper you've got there?

FLORRIE. Yes.

MRS. PETTER. Is the verdict out on that taxi driver case?

FLORRIE. No, not yet. Just the judge's summing up.

MRS. PETTER. Oh!

FLORRIE. You know, I don't see what use judges are. They don't seem to say anything useful or tell the jury what they ought to do.

MRS. PETTER. How'd you mean?

FLORRIE. Well, listen to this, "Whereas Sir Luke has stated in the case for the prosecution", etcetera, etcetera, "In which case the prisoner is undoubtedly guilty – but at the same time you must take into account the contention of the defence, that the prisoner had not the necessary knowledge to," etcetera, etcetera, "In which case you will have no alternative but to acquit the accused." Why doesn't he tell them if the prisoner's done it or not?

MRS. PETTER. Perhaps he doesn't know.

FLORRIE. Well, he's the judge, isn't he? Fancy if you had weather forecasts like that.

(She speaks in an exaggerated voice.)

If the weather improves tomorrow, it will be warm and sunny. If, on the other hand, the depression spreads, it will be wet and cold.

MRS. PETTER. Might as well have a weather forecast like that, for all the good they are. Ruined my best hat last Sunday, listening to what they said.

FLORRIE. Now, I like a man like Sir Luke Enderby, the one who was prosecuting. Gave it to the jury hot and strong, he did. Beautiful it was, especially that bit about doing their duty, however painful, and how people like the prisoner were a menace to society.

MRS. PETTER. I remember Sir Luke Enderby in that blonde on the beach murder.

FLORRIE. Yes, that's the man.

MRS. PETTER. All about those poor girls being lured to their death by a sadistic murderer. That was a good murder, that was. I don't like this taxi murder so much.

FLORRIE. No, it's a bit dull.

MRS. PETTER. But of course, he did it all right.

FLORRIE. Yes, but he looks such an insignificant little chap. Now Garfield, the blonde on the beach murderer, he was really good looking.

MRS. PETTER. Now you be careful, Florrie.

FLORRIE. Why?

MRS. PETTER. That's what all those poor girls thought – they let him pick them up as easy as easy. You be careful of these flash, good looking fellows that try to pick girls up.

(A knock at the door is heard.)

FLORRIE. That must be Mrs. Keene.

(She calls.)

Come in!

*(The door opens. **JULIA** speaks in a charming voice.)*

JULIA. Good evening, Mrs. Petter.

MRS. PETTER. Good evening, Mrs. Keene.

JULIA. Good evening, Florrie.

FLORRIE. Evening.

JULIA. I wonder if I might use your telephone Mrs. Petter?

MRS. PETTER. Why, certainly, Mrs. Keene. Come in.

JULIA. Thank you.
MRS. PETTER. Do you want the book?
JULIA. No, I know the number.

(There is a slight pause.)

It isn't foggy outside, is it, Florrie?

FLORRIE. Just a bit – not much.

*(**JULIA** is heard dialling.)*

JULIA. It will be all right in the country, I hope.
MRS. PETTER. You going to the country?
JULIA. Just for the weekend.
MRS. PETTER. Well, I'll just – come on, Florrie.

(The door closes.)

JULIA. Hullo? Is that nineteen Chishold Gardens?... Can I speak to Sir Luke Enderby please?... Oh, I see... No, no message... No name...

(Her voice fades as we flip to the other side of the call.)

I'll ring again later...

*(There is a click as **HAYWARD** replaces the receiver. His voice is elderly and rather gloomy.)*

HAYWARD. No message. No name. She'll ring again later. Another of them!

(The front door bell is heard ringing.)

There's the front door. First the telephone, then the door! If it's not one thing, it's another.

*(The front door opens and the sound of a London residential square is heard. **SUSAN** is a brisk young woman with an astringent manner.)*

SUSAN. Good afternoon, Hayward.
HAYWARD. Good afternoon, Miss Warren.

(The front door closes.)

HAYWARD. Lady Enderby isn't in yet, but she's expecting you.

SUSAN. Oh, that's all right. Sir Luke's still at the Old Bailey, I suppose?

HAYWARD. Yes madam, will you come in to the drawing room?

(There is a slight pause. They are heard moving through the house.)

SUSAN. How's the rheumatism, Hayward?

HAYWARD. It's been bad lately, what with the telephone and answering the door.

SUSAN. Oh I'm sorry.

HAYWARD. These large houses are very inconvenient. I said to her ladyship only yesterday, how different it would be if we could have a nice flat.

SUSAN. A nice flat wouldn't take all Lady Enderby's nice things.

HAYWARD. Ye-e-es, her ladyship has got some nice things. She's out at the sale rooms this afternoon.

SUSAN. Oh, so that's where she is! There'll be even more lovely things presently. No hope of that nice flat, Hayward.

HAYWARD. No.

SUSAN. It's more likely to be an even larger house.

HAYWARD. Oh, don't suggest that, madam. Would you care for the evening paper?

SUSAN. No thanks. I'll amuse myself with a book.

HAYWARD. Right, madam.

SUSAN. What's this one? *Ogden on Criminal Jurisprudence.* That's Sir Luke's, I suppose.

HAYWARD. Yes.

SUSAN. A bit heavy for me.

(The front door opens and closes. Someone is heard approaching.)

HAYWARD. That's either her ladyship or Sir Luke.

SIR LUKE. Well, well, look who's here!

SUSAN. Hello Luke.

SIR LUKE. Lovely to see you, Susan. Where's Marion?

SUSAN. At the sale rooms.

SIR LUKE. That will mean more Buhl cabinets and Aubusson carpets and Chinese bronzes! *(Quietly.)* Any telephone messages for me, Hayward?

HAYWARD. A lady rang up just now, sir. She didn't leave her name or a message.

*(**SIR LUKE** speaks rather falsely.)*

SIR LUKE. I wonder who that could be.

SUSAN. *(Ironically.)* I suppose you couldn't possibly guess.

HAYWARD. Shall I bring in tea, sir?

SIR LUKE. Yes, please.

HAYWARD. Thank you, sir.

(The door closes softly.)

SUSAN. Do you encourage them to ring you up here?

SIR LUKE. I don't know what you mean!

SUSAN. Come off it, darling. I mean your various lady friends.

SIR LUKE. Aren't you well aware, Susan, that you're the only girl I've ever loved?

SUSAN. I'm aware that you're never at a loss for an answer! How did the case go?

SIR LUKE. The case?

SUSAN. Haven't you just come from the Old Bailey?

SIR LUKE. Oh, that. Guilty. Couldn't have been any other verdict. Why the jury wanted to stay out two hours and a half, I can't imagine.

SUSAN. No indeed. After your masterly speech the jury should have brought him in guilty without bothering to leave the box!

SIR LUKE. After all, he did shoot the taxi driver.

SUSAN. Yes, I can't pretend there has really been a grave miscarriage of justice, although I always try to.

SIR LUKE. Why?

SUSAN. Just to annoy you.

SIR LUKE. Why do you want to get your knife into me? What have I done to you?

SUSAN. Nothing. You just look so completely sure of yourself and so thoroughly pleased with yourself!

(The front door opens and closes. Someone is heard approaching.)

MARION. Darlings, am I terribly late?

SUSAN. How are you, Marion?

MARION. Susan dear, how nice to see you.

(The chinking of a tea tray is heard.)

Why on earth didn't you start tea? Oh good, Hayward's bringing it now.

SIR LUKE. *(Quietly.)* Were there any letters for me, Hayward?

HAYWARD. In your study, sir.

SIR LUKE. I'd better just have a look at them.

(The door closes.)

MARION. Milk, Susan? You don't have sugar, I know.

SUSAN. Thank you.

MARION. I hope you haven't been waiting very long?

SUSAN. Oh no, I've been improving my mind with this book.

MARION. *(Amused.)* My goodness, not *Criminal Jurisprudence*?

SUSAN. Does Luke really read this sort of thing for pleasure?

MARION. Not exactly pleasure. Just to look up some special point.

SUSAN. I know the sort of thing. Doublechuck v. Fathead in the reign of Charles the First – and for some inscrutable reason it affects the case of the Crown v. Dreary Product Limited today. I really think the law is extraordinary!

MARION. I must say that sometimes it doesn't seem very sensible. Bread and butter, dear?

SUSAN. Thanks.

(There is a slight pause.)

Luke's looking frightfully pleased with himself.

MARION. I suppose the verdict was guilty. He said it was a certainty.

SUSAN. Naturally. He was just slightly annoyed at the jury being impertinent enough to stay out two hours and a half. Lèse majesté after his speech for the prosecution.

MARION. *(Hurt.)* Susan darling, that's not very kind.

SUSAN. Darling, it was abominable of me. But I would simply hate to stand in the dock charged with murder and have Luke prosecuting.

MARION. But you'd like it if he were defending you?

SUSAN. Perhaps. But he never does seem to defend people.

MARION. Well anyway, if you were innocent, you'd have nothing to be afraid of.

SUSAN. Wouldn't I?

MARION. Innocent people are always acquitted.

SUSAN. Are they? I wonder.

MARION. Of course.

SUSAN. I wish I was as sure about it as you are.

(The door opens.)

MARION. Ask Luke.

SIR LUKE. Ask Luke what?

SUSAN. Are innocent people always acquitted?

SIR LUKE. No need to worry about that. The real worry is that some cold-blooded murderer gets off scot-free because some sentimental women on the jury like his face.

SUSAN. The blonde on the beach? Garfield?

MARION. But he wasn't acquitted.

SIR LUKE. No, but he might have been. There were four women on the jury.

SUSAN. Extraordinary how women fell for that man. How many women had he actually killed?

SIR LUKE. Certainly two –

SUSAN. The original blonde at Bexhill and that girl at Weymouth?

SIR LUKE. Probably three – and possibly a good many more!

SUSAN. He was terribly good looking. Mad, I suppose?

SIR LUKE. Oh no, not in the legal sense. He knew what he was doing all right.

MARION. *(Plaintively.)* Couldn't you two possibly stop talking about murders?

SIR LUKE. Sorry, darling. Tell me what you've been doing? Sotheby's?

MARION. Christie's. My dears, I got the most lovely pair of Chinese pictures on glass. Absolutely exquisite.

SIR LUKE. And where are you going to put them?

MARION. I'm going to hang them on that wall over there. There were a lot of dealers after them – they ran me up rather high.

SIR LUKE. Just as well I make a bit at the bar.

SUSAN. You hang people and Marion hangs pictures!

MARION. But they really are unique.

SUSAN. So is this house – absolutely perfect, darling.

SIR LUKE. It should be, when you consider that Marion's house comes first, and Marion's husband a long way after.

MARION. What nonsense! I'm the most devoted wife.

SIR LUKE. You're the most wonderful wife a man ever had.

SUSAN. Twitter, twitter, coo coo! Listen to the turtledoves – excuse my vulgar noises.

MARION. More tea, Luke?

SIR LUKE. No time. I must be off. Got to catch a train to Liverpool.

SUSAN. Why Liverpool?

SIR LUKE. Work to be done.

MARION. Oh, what a bore. Really, dear, you ought to have some time off. You work much too hard.

SIR LUKE. I'll have a real rest one of these days. Goodbye, darling, take care of yourself.

MARION. Bye, dear.

SIR LUKE. Bye, Susan. Be good.

SUSAN. Wouldn't that come better from me to you?

SIR LUKE. Now then Susan. I must run. I'll miss my train.

(There is a pause. The front door bangs closed. **SUSAN**'s *tone changes completely.)*

SUSAN. Gone to meet some woman, I suppose?

(All the brightness vanishes from **MARION**'s *voice. It sounds dead and tired.)*

MARION. Probably.

SUSAN. How you stand it I don't know, Marion.

MARION. After a time one doesn't mind so much.

SUSAN. I wonder. How long have you been married?

MARION. Ten years.

SUSAN. And practically all the time Luke has been chasing after some woman or other?

MARION. Oh, not on the honeymoon. I think he was absolutely faithful on the honeymoon.

SUSAN. That's very nearly the most cutting thing I've ever heard you say! Haven't you ever considered leaving him?

MARION. I've considered it, yes.

SUSAN. Tell me, do you care for him still?

MARION. Oh my dear, so many things go to make up a marriage. There are the boys. They're devoted to him and he's an excellent father. And he is always kind and charming to me. I think he's really very fond of me. All those women don't really mean anything, you know. These infatuations never last. It's just – well – weakness on his part. Any good looking woman has only to throw herself at his head and he accepts the challenge.

SUSAN. Whose challenge is he accepting at this minute?

MARION. I think this is a new one. By all the signs.

SUSAN. Any idea who she is?

MARION. None at all.

SUSAN. I wonder where they're meeting? Certainly not Liverpool. I wonder...

(Fade.)

Scene Two

(The noises of a train station are heard.)

FIRST VOICE. Could you tell me what platform for Henley?

SECOND VOICE. I'm sorry I've no idea. Perhaps a porter could help you.

THIRD VOICE. Could you manage a corner seat?

PORTER. Well, I'll try but we're pretty full up.

SIR LUKE. Julia, dearest! You've really come! I was so afraid you wouldn't.

*(**JULIA**'s voice is deep with emotion.)*

JULIA. What a wonderful place Paddington Station is. I never realised it before.

SIR LUKE. Julia…

JULIA. I telephoned, but you weren't in.

SIR LUKE. I heard someone had rung up. I was terrified that it was to say you'd changed your mind.

JULIA. As if I would.

SIR LUKE. Oh Julia, how beautiful you are. I do love you!

JULIA. *(Shakily.)* You can't say things like that in Paddington Station. Besides we shall miss our train.

SIR LUKE. I don't even know where we're going.

JULIA. That makes it more exciting, doesn't it? Come along, we must hurry. It's number five.

SIR LUKE. Where are we going?

JULIA. The station's called Warning Halt.

SIR LUKE. Warning Halt? Never heard of it.

JULIA. Nobody has. Come on, hurry.

SIR LUKE. It sounds completely the back of beyond.

JULIA. Oh, we'll miss the train. Run!

PORTER. Stand away there!

(A train is heard whistling and puffing smoke as it pulls out of the station. Fade.)

Scene Three

(The screech of brakes is heard as the train draws into a country platform.)

PORTER. *(Calling.)* Warning Halt, Warning Halt.

JULIA. Thank goodness, no fog here.

SIR LUKE. Yes, thank goodness. Do we get a taxi?

JULIA. Oh no, we walk. My cottage is only about three minutes away.

PORTER. Tickets, please. Thank you. Good evening.

JULIA. Good evening. No, this way – there's a footpath across the field.

SIR LUKE. Oh, it's a heavenly night. Just look at those clouds chasing each other across the moon.

JULIA. Come on, you old poet. It's too cold to stand stargazing.

SIR LUKE. You know, I never knew you had a cottage in the country.

JULIA. But then you don't know much about me, do you?

SIR LUKE. I know that when I saw you across the room at the Ritz that day, and you smiled at me, that the whole world changed. Just over a fortnight ago. It seems a lifetime. And now, at last –

JULIA. Dearest, you don't mind, do you, coming here to the cottage? I did so hate the idea of a hotel for us. It seemed so sordid – the subterfuges, false names, perhaps meeting someone who might recognise us. Oh, I couldn't bear it. You do understand, don't you?

SIR LUKE. Of course I do, dearest. I love you even more for being so sensitive. All that matters is that we should be together. I don't care how primitive the place is.

JULIA. *(Playfully.)* I'd have you know that my cottage is not primitive. It has every creature comfort. Hot water and electric light, and to cheer us through the beastly rationing, the best to eat that the local black market can provide.

SIR LUKE. Ha, sounds wonderful.

(Fade.)

Scene Four

(The sound of **JULIA** *searching her handbag for keys.)*

JULIA. Here we are. Let me find the key. I've got it.

(The front door unlocks.)

Just a minute. I'll switch on the light. There, how do you like my retreat?

SIR LUKE. It's delightful. What a charming room.

(The door closes.)

JULIA. I hoped you'd like it. Just set a match to the fire. I'll bring in supper. It's all ready.

(A match strikes and the fire begins to crackle.)

SIR LUKE. What a wonderful woman you are, Julia. Even your fire lights and burns up at once. Isn't that supposed to be a sign that your lover is true to you? What a lovely thing a fire is on an autumn evening.

(He calls.)

Julia?

JULIA. *(Offstage.)* Coming!

SIR LUKE. *(Calling.)* You're a wonderful woman.

JULIA. *(Offstage.)* What? Here we are.

(The sound of dishes being put on a table is heard.)

What were you saying?

SIR LUKE. *(Ardently.)* That you're the most wonderful creature in the world. There's something different about you from any other woman I've ever met.

JULIA. *(Mockingly.)* And how many women have you said that to?

SIR LUKE. *(Amorously.)* Darling...

JULIA. No, no, Luke. Be good. Supper. Definitely supper, and though I say it myself, rather a good supper.

SIR LUKE. By Jove, cold duck. And is that pâté?

JULIA. It is.

SIR LUKE. And do my eyes deceive me, is that immense yellow pyramid real butter?

>   (**JULIA** *speaks in a rather peculiar voice.*)

JULIA. Butter in a lordly dish...

SIR LUKE. *(Gaily.)* It sounds quite Biblical.

JULIA. Does it? *(Gravely.)* Is my lord satisfied with what his servant has set before him?

SIR LUKE. *(Amorously.)* You enchanting creature. Julia...

JULIA. *(Playfully.)* No, not now. Supper. I insist on stern self-control till after supper.

>   *(They both laugh. Fade.)*

Scene Five

(The fire is heard blazing.)

JULIA. Now then, sit in the big armchair. I'll put your coffee by you here.

SIR LUKE. Oh darling. What a perfect meal that was. And now, perfect coffee! Damned few women can make good coffee. It seems incredible, Julia, that a fortnight ago I'd never even seen you.

JULIA. I've known you by sight a much longer time. You were pointed out to me.

SIR LUKE. Really?

JULIA. You're a very celebrated man.

SIR LUKE. Nonsense.

JULIA. You're the most famous counsel in England. Doesn't it ever upset you to feel that your eloquence and your power has got some poor wretch hanged?

SIR LUKE. Not if the poor wretch richly deserves it.

JULIA. Supposing he doesn't? Supposing he's innocent?

SIR LUKE. I don't think that what you so romantically call, my eloquence, or my legal tricks, have ever hanged an innocent man.

JULIA. No.

SIR LUKE. There's not usually much doubt about murderers who get convicted. Trouble is that occasionally a fellow gets off who's as guilty as hell.

JULIA. Garfield didn't get off...

SIR LUKE. The blonde on the beach murderer?

JULIA. Yes.

SIR LUKE. Oh, no doubt about him.

JULIA. But supposing he wasn't guilty. There wasn't really very much evidence against him, was there?

SIR LUKE. My dear girl, the police had been after Garfield for months. There had been two other girls before that, remember. The police knew quite well who had done it, but I believe his wife always cooked up the most wonderful alibi for him. Not that a wife's word goes very far – but in the absence of definite evidence of his having been seen with the girls near the times of the murders, they couldn't risk charging him before.

JULIA. That's what I say. There wasn't really any evidence against him.

SIR LUKE. Now look here, Julia, talking strict facts – not legal tender – but plain, off the record, common sense.

JULIA. Well.

SIR LUKE. Garfield is friendly with girl number one. She's strangled. Garfield has a date with girl number two. She's found dead. Then he carries on with girl number three and she's murdered. Can't be coincidence. The fellow's got a sex complex and can't resist killing these girls.

JULIA. Then why didn't they say he was insane?

SIR LUKE. Because he wasn't. He knew well enough what he was doing and what would happen to him if he got caught. And he was so extraordinarily clever that it wasn't easy to catch him.

JULIA. The judge's summing up was in his favour.

SIR LUKE. Ye-e-s, the actual evidence was thin. But it wasn't needed. The jury took one look at Garfield and made up their minds.

JULIA. No, they listened to you. You got him convicted.

SIR LUKE. Well, perhaps I did my bit. He was a nice looking chap. A plausible way with him. Couple of women on the jury were looking quite sentimental about him. I had to smash that.

JULIA. Women have very sound instincts.

SIR LUKE. Now don't give me that old stuff about a woman's instinct. Women are notorious for liking wrong 'uns. Look at that wife of his. Blindly devoted to him, apparently. If she hadn't been in hospital with typhoid at the time of the trial, she might somehow have pulled the trick again. I never saw her, but I believe she was an amazingly good liar – or so Inspector Garrod told me. When she swore to him that Garfield had been at home with her at the crucial times, you couldn't help but believe her. Amazing creatures, women.

(He gives a sharp exclamation of pain.)

JULIA. What's the matter?

SIR LUKE. Ooh – got cramp in my leg. Ah, that's better.

JULIA. Have some more coffee.

SIR LUKE. Thank you, darling. What a meal! You're a wonderful woman, Julia. "Butter in a lordly dish" – now where does that come from? The Bible? Esther? No, it isn't Esther.

JULIA. Don't you remember?

SIR LUKE. I'll get it in a minute.

(He gives another exclamation of pain.)

Ooh – funny this cramp. I feel quite stiff. What were we talking about?

JULIA. Killing...

SIR LUKE. Oh, yes. Garfield. If that man had been able to leave women alone, he'd be alive today.

JULIA. But some men can't leave women alone, can they? *(Significantly.)* Can they, Luke?

SIR LUKE. I'm fond of women, I admit it. But this time, with you, it's something quite different.

JULIA. Yes, one always has to say that. It's expected. What does your wife feel about these excursions of yours?

SIR LUKE. *(Cautiously.)* I think we'd better leave my wife out of it.

JULIA. I'm sorry.

(There is a pause.)

SIR LUKE. "Butter in a lordly dish" – funny how that keeps running in my mind. Why do I feel those words have got a – a kind of sinister sound to them? I wish I could remember.

JULIA. Would these help you to remember?

SIR LUKE. I can't see what it is you're holding up there. What's the matter with my eyes? I can't focus properly.

JULIA. It's a hammer and some nails.

SIR LUKE. *(Amused.)* You extraordinary woman. What do you want a hammer and nails for?

JULIA. Perhaps to hang up a picture on the wall.

SIR LUKE. At this time of night? Really, Julia, what a barbarous idea!

JULIA. Yes, it is rather barbarous. But then women can be barbarous.

(There is a pause.)

It was, of course, a grave breach of hospitality.

SIR LUKE. What was?

JULIA. What Jael did to Sisera.

SIR LUKE. Jael? Sisera? Of course, I've got it! Jael and Sisera. She's the one who brought him butter in a lordly dish and then hammered a nail through his forehead.

(His voice changes suddenly.)

A nail...

JULIA. What's the matter, Luke?

SIR LUKE. *(Thickly.)* I – look here – damn, I'm stiff and cramped all over. My eyes are playing me tricks – all misty. I can't get up!

JULIA. No, you can't get up. That's the result of the drug in your coffee.

SIR LUKE. Drug in the coffee? What do you mean, Julia?

JULIA. The drug I put in your coffee. Do you know who I am, Luke?

SIR LUKE. You're Julia.

JULIA. Julia, yes. But my other name?

SIR LUKE. Keene. Julia Keene.

JULIA. No, I took the name of Keene. My own name was rather too conspicuous. I'm Julia Garfield, Luke.

SIR LUKE. What? Garfield... Garfield?!

JULIA. I'm Henry Garfield's wife. That is, I should be Henry Garfield's wife – but for you. Because of you and your eloquence and your legal tricks, I'm Henry Garfield's widow.

SIR LUKE. *(Drowsily.)* What's all this? What are you up to?... You got me here...

JULIA. It wasn't very difficult. I knew your reputation. You fall for women very easily, don't you, Luke?

SIR LUKE. I – must – get – out – of – here –

JULIA. I loved Henry Garfield.

SIR LUKE. I – must – get – out – of – here!

JULIA. I loved Henry Garfield. You killed him.

SIR LUKE. Henry Garfield was – a murderer –

JULIA. Oh no, he wasn't. I killed those women.

SIR LUKE. You?

JULIA. It wasn't Henry's fault. He just fell easily for women – like you. They beckoned and he followed. But I wasn't like your wife, content to sit at home and buy pretty things and shut her eyes. I wasn't going to share Henry with any woman – silly, giggling little blondes! They didn't giggle when I'd finished with them.

(**JULIA** *laughs darkly.*)

SIR LUKE. Stop that.

JULIA. Yes, I must stop it. There are things to do.

SIR LUKE. You're mad... You're mad!

JULIA. *(Calmly.)* Not in the legal sense. I know quite well what I'm going to do.

SIR LUKE. *(Frenzied.)* Put that hammer down – go away from me! God, I can't move! Keep away from me! Marion... Marion...! Keep her away from me! Keep away... Keep away...!

(*A groan is heard. There is a slight pause then the sound of a nail being hammered into something soft.* **JULIA** *laughs madly.*)

End of Play

THE AGATHA CHRISTIE COLLECTION

Agatha Christie is regarded as the most successful female playwright of all time. Her illustrious dramatic career spans forty-two years, countless acclaimed original plays, several renowned novels adapted for stage, and numerous collections of thrilling one-act plays. Testament to Christie's longevity, these plays continue to engage great artists and enthral audiences today.

Since the première of her first play in 1930 the world of theatre has changed immeasurably, and so has the way plays are published and performed. Embarking upon a two-year project, Agatha Christie Limited sought to re-open Christie's distinguished body of dramatic work, looking to both original manuscripts and the most recent publications to create a "remastered" edition of each play. Each new text would contain only the words of Agatha Christie (or adaptors she personally worked with) and all extraneous materials that might come between the interpreter and the playwright would be removed, ultimately bringing the flavor and content of the texts closer to what the author would have delivered to the rehearsal room. Each new edition would then be specifically tailored to the needs and requirements of the professional twenty-first century artist.

The result is The Collection.

Whether in a classic revival or new approach, The Collection has been purposely assembled for the contemporary theatre professional. The choice and combination of plays offers something for all tastes and kinds of performance with the skill, imagination and genius of Agatha Christie's work now waiting to be explored anew in theatre.

For more information on The Collection, please visit
agathachristielimited.com/licensing/stage/browse-by-play

Milton Keynes UK
Ingram Content Group UK Ltd.
UKHW021939281223
435011UK00012B/199